שמע ישראל שמע ישראל

00004 296 CLA

AYLESBURY CC
OXFORD ROAD
AYLESBURY, B
Tel: 01296 5885

Please return book on or before last date stamped below

Evans

שמע ישראל   שמע ישראל

Notes for Teachers and Parents

Pages 6/7 Jews believe in One God, the Creator of the Universe, who is also a personal God. The Torah, which was revealed by God to Moses on Mount Sinai, contains the central teachings of Judaism. Jews serve God by carrying out the laws contained in the Torah; belief in God has to be complemented by righteous actions. There are some 13.5 million Jews in the world today, of whom about 285,000 live in the UK. Jews see themselves as an extended family, rather than a race or a religion. Family life is of key importance in the transmission of Jewish traditions and values.

Pages 8/9 Observant Jews do not work or travel on Shabbat, which is a day set aside for spiritual renewal and family life. On Friday evening family and friends gather at home for a festive meal. The two special loaves of bread, called challah (pronounced hallah) represent the double portion of manna which God provided for the Israelites in the wilderness on the eve of Shabbat and festivals, see Exodus 16:22/26.

Pages 10/11 Shabbat ends at nightfall on Saturday with a ceremony called havdalah, meaning separation. Lighting the plaited havdalah candle is the first act of work after Shabbat. The overflowing cup of wine is a symbol of joy. The spices symbolize the 'sweetness' of Shabbat which Jews wish to take with them into the working week. The play of light and shadow on the cupped hands held out towards the candle flame is a symbolic parallel of the distinction between Shabbat and the weekdays.

Pages 12/13 Zoë's family worships in an Orthodox synagogue in which men and women sit separately. The males cover their head with a kippah (skullcap) as a sign of respect for God and wear a tallit (prayer shawl). Married women are also required to cover their hair. The Ark, which is the cupboard containing the Torah scrolls, is at the front of the synagogue and is generally only opened to remove or return a scroll.

Pages 14/15 The Torah scroll is handwritten by a trained scribe on parchment made from the skins of kosher animals. Both photos show boys celebrating their Bar Mitzvah (a Jewish boy's coming of age at 13 years old), one in London, the other at the Western Wall in Jerusalem. This is all that remains of the Temple today and is a place of prayer and pilgrimage for Jewish people.

Pages 16/17 The mezuzah is a small handwritten parchment scroll containing part of the Shema, one of the most important Jewish prayers. It is rolled up, placed in a protective case and fixed to the right-hand doorpost of every room in Jewish homes, synagogues and shops, except the bathroom and toilet, in response to the command: 'you shall write them (these words) on the doorposts of your house' (Deuteronomy 6:9).

Pages 18/19 Many children who do not go to Jewish schools attend supplementary classes which are generally held in the synagogue on Sunday mornings. The curriculum includes the study of Hebrew, Torah, Jewish history, customs and celebrations. The children also learn about the mitzvot (commandments, singular mitzvah) which

Jews are expected to fulfil, such as Tzedaka, the obligation to give to people in need. The Hebrew writing on Zoë's money box says Tzedaka.

Pages 20/21 The main celebration of the festival of Pesach (Passover) is the seder meal when the story of the Exodus from Egypt is read from a book called the hagadah. The seder was designed as an educational experience for children. Zoë can be seen asking four specified questions about the seder, traditionally the role of the youngest child present. The seder plate contains symbolic foods, such as a roasted egg and roasted bone. Zoë and her father are dipping bitter herbs (horseradish) symbolizing the bitterness of slavery into a sweet paste called haroset. Notice the beautifully embroidered cloth covering the matzah (unleavened bread).

Pages 22/23 The basic regulations about kosher food are laid down in Leviticus 11 with regard to the animals, birds and fish that Jews are permitted to eat. In addition, animals and birds must be killed by a prescribed painless method and the blood removed. Jews are not allowed to eat meat and dairy foods at the same meal.

Pages 24/25 Sukkot is a time of thanksgiving for food and for shelter. The sukkah calls to mind the temporary dwellings used by the Israelites while wandering in the wilderness. The most important part of the structure is the roof which is made of cut branches and must be open to the sky. Children enjoy decorating the sukkah with fruit and with their own artwork. Simchat Torah is the festival at the end of Sukkot when Jews celebrate the completion and immediate recommencement of the annual cycle of Torah readings in the synagogue.

Pages 26/27 Hanukkah commemorates the deliverance of the Jews from religious persecution in the 2nd century BCE and the subsequent rededication of the Temple in Jerusalem. It is celebrated by lighting oil lamps or candles, one light on the first night, two the second and so on up to eight. Presents are exchanged and there are special Hanukkah foods and games. Jewish people light a yahrzeit or memorial candle each year on the anniversary of the death of close relatives. The candle burns for 24 hours and symbolizes the departed soul. It is also lit on Yom Kippur, the Day of Atonement, the holiest day of the Jewish year.

Pages 28/29 Jewish couples get married under a canopy called a huppah (pronounced hoo-pa) which symbolizes the Jewish home which they will build together. The canopy is often decorated with flowers. Baby boys receive their Jewish names when they are circumcised at eight days of age. In Orthodox communities girls are given their Jewish names when the father recites a blessing in the synagogue on the Shabbat following their birth. In Progressive communities, both boys and girls have a naming ceremony in the synagogue on a Shabbat morning.

The Hebrew calligraphy at the top of each page is Shema Yisrael, 'Hear O Israel' (read from right to left), the first two words of the Shema, one of the most important Jewish prayers: 'Hear O Israel, the Eternal our God, the Eternal is One' (Deuteronomy 6:4). It has been specially commissioned for this book and handwritten in a traditional script.

שְׁמַע יִשְׂרָאֵל שְׁמַע יִשְׂרָאֵל

Hello! My name is Zoë.

שְׁמַע יִשְׂרָאֵל שְׁמַע יִשְׂרָאֵל

My family and I are Jewish.
Jews believe in one God who
is the Creator of the world.
God cares for everyone.

שְׁמַע יִשְׂרָאֵל שְׁמַע יִשְׂרָאֵל שְׁמַע יִשְׂרָאֵל

Every Friday evening we celebrate the start of Shabbat. Shabbat is a day of rest, fun and prayer for Jewish people.

שמע ישראל שמע ישראל

We light candles.
We drink wine and
share sweet white bread.

How long does Shabbat last?

It lasts until Saturday night.
At the end of Shabbat
we light another candle
and smell sweet spices.

שמע ישראל שמע ישראל

We hold our hands towards the candle. The flame feels warm.

שמע ישראל שמע ישראל

Where do Jews meet for worship?

We go to synagogue to pray to God with our family and friends.
We go on Shabbat and on festival days.

שְׁמַע יִשְׂרָאֵל שְׁמַע יִשְׂרָאֵל

This is the rabbi, the leader of our Jewish community. He is holding one of the Torah scrolls.

שמע ישראל שמע ישראל

What is a Torah scroll?

A Torah scroll contains the first five books of the Bible. It is written in Hebrew, the language Jewish people use for worship.

שמע ישראל שמע ישראל

This Torah scroll is in
Jerusalem, in Israel.
Jerusalem is a special
place for Jewish people.

It is a mezuzah. It has words
from the Torah.
It is kept in a small case.

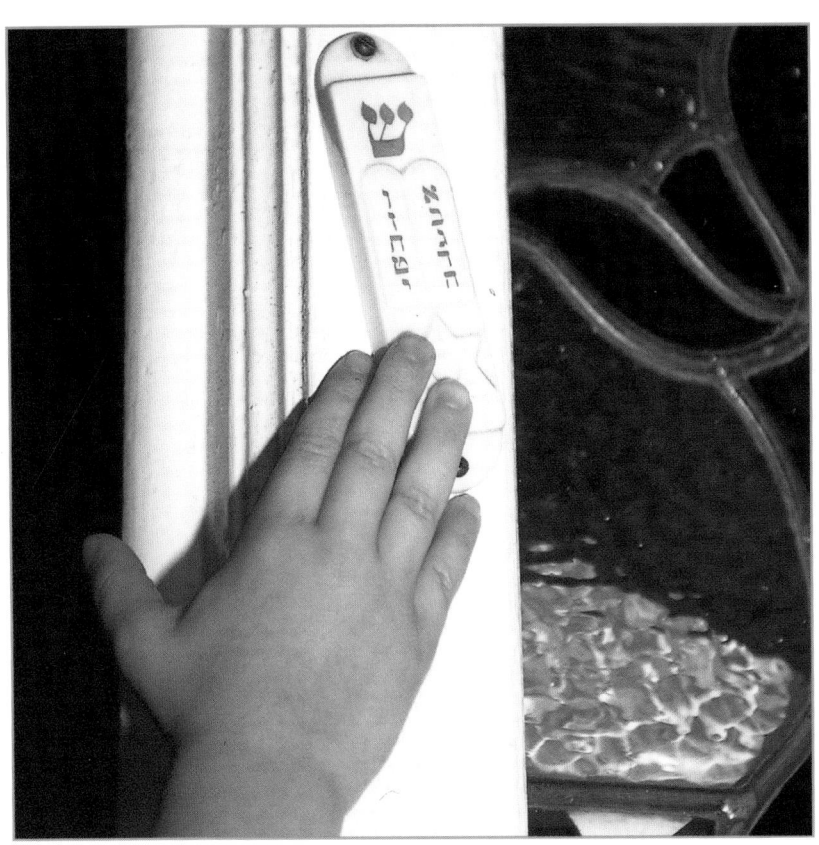

Jewish people put a mezuzah
on doorposts in their house.
Some Jews touch it as they
go in and out of their home.

שְׁמַע יִשְׂרָאֵל שְׁמַע יִשְׂרָאֵל

> *Do you have lessons about your faith?*

I go to Sunday classes to learn how to live as a Jew.

שְׁמַע יִשְׂרָאֵל שְׁמַע יִשְׂרָאֵל

Jews have to help people
in need.
I help by giving some money
each week. I put the money
in a special box.

שְׁמַע יִשְׂרָאֵל שְׁמַע יִשְׂרָאֵל

> *What is your favourite festival?*

I like Pesach, because all my family are together for a special meal called the seder.

We eat special foods when we tell the story of how God helped the Jews escape from Egypt long ago.

שְׁמַע יִשְׂרָאֵל   שְׁמַע יִשְׂרָאֵל

What kinds of food do Jewish people eat?

The Torah tells us what foods we can eat and how to cook them. These are called kosher foods.

שְׁמַע יִשְׂרָאֵל שְׁמַע יִשְׂרָאֵל

At Rosh Hashanah, we eat
slices of apple dipped
in honey.
We pray for
a sweet and
happy new
year.

23

During the week of Sukkot, we eat all our meals outside in a hut called a sukkah.

שְׁמַע יִשְׂרָאֵל שְׁמַע יִשְׂרָאֵל

On Simchat Torah we sing
and dance with the Torah
scrolls to show how happy
we are to have the Torah.

Tonight is the sixth night of the festival.

We light an extra candle on our hanukiah on each of the eight nights of Hanukkah.

שְׁמַע יִשְׂרָאֵל שְׁמַע יִשְׂרָאֵל

Why is your grandmother lighting this candle?

My grandparents light a special candle each year to remember their parents on the day that they died.

שְׁמַע יִשְׂרָאֵל שְׁמַע יִשְׂרָאֵל שְׁמַע יִשְׂרָאֵל

What about the happy times in your family?

Jewish people like to celebrate together. I was a bridesmaid at my cousin's wedding. She married in a synagogue.

שְׁמַע יִשְׂרָאֵל שְׁמַע יִשְׂרָאֵל

This is my cousin's baby.
It is his naming ceremony.
We all said a special prayer
to welcome him into the
Jewish community.

שְׁמַע יִשְׂרָאֵל שְׁמַע יִשְׂרָאֵל

Glossary

hanukiah - A lamp with nine branches used during Hanukkah.
Hanukkah - A festival of lights.
Pesach - A spring festival when Jews remember their escape from slavery in Egypt.
rabbi - A Jewish religious teacher and leader.
Rosh Hashanah - The Jewish New Year.
seder - A special meal in Jewish homes on Pesach
Shabbat - The Jewish day of rest and celebration which lasts from sunset on Friday until nightfall on Saturday.
Sukkot - An autumn harvest festival.
Torah - The first five books of the Bible.

Index

Bible, the 14

candles 9,10,11,26,27

festivals 12, 20-21,23-26

God 7,12

Hebrew 14

Jerusalem 15

kosher food 22

mezuzah 16,17

naming ceremony 29

rabbi 13

Shabbat 8,10,12

synagogue 12,28

Torah 13,14,15,16,22,25

wedding 28